Leading at School

John C. Maxwell
Leadership Books for Students

(Based on *Developing the Leader Within You*)

Leading from the Lockers:
Student Edition

ISBN 0-8499-7722-3

Leading from the Lockers:
Guided Journal

ISBN 0-8499-7723-1

The PowerPak Series

Leading Your Sports Team

ISBN 0-8499-7725-8

Leading in Your Youth Group

ISBN 0-8499-7726-6

Leading at School

ISBN 0-8499-7724-X

Leading As a Friend

ISBN 0-8499-7727-4

"These books are outstanding. John Maxwell's leadership principles have been communicated in a way that any student can understand and practice. Take them and go make a difference in your world."

—DR. TIM ELMORE,
Vice President of Leadership Development, EQUIP;
Author of *Nurturing the Leader in Your Child*

Leading at
School

by
John C. Maxwell

with

Monica Hall

Tommy nelson®
Thomas Nelson, Inc. • Nashville

POWERPAK SERIES: LEADING AT SCHOOL

Based on John C. Maxwell's *Developing the Leader Within You.*

Published in Nashville, Tennessee, by Tommy Nelson®, a division of Thomas Nelson, Inc.

Special thanks to Ron Luce and Teen Mania for providing research materials for this book.

Unless otherwise indicated, Scripture quotations are from the *International Children's Bible, New Century Version*, copyright © 1983, 1986, 1988.

Scripture quotations marked (NKJV) are from THE NEW KING JAMES VERSION of the Bible, copyright © 1979, 1980, 1982, Thomas Nelson, Inc., Publishers.

Library of Congress Cataloging-in-Publication Data

Maxwell, John C., 1947–
    Leading at school / originated by John C. Maxwell; adapted by Monica Hall.
      p. cm. — (PowerPak collection)
    ISBN 0-8499-7724-X
    1. Leadership—Juvenile literature. 2. Leadership—Religious aspects—Christianity—Juvenile literature. 3. Students—Conduct of life—Juvenile literature. I. Hall, Monica. II. Title. III. Series.

HM1261 .M39 2001
303.3'4—dc21

2001030742

Contents

1
What? Me Lead?!
(You're Kidding, Right?)

Yes, *you*! God could be calling you—right now—to become a leader at *your* school. Are you listening? Because this is one call you don't want to miss!

"Why *me*?" you may be wondering (looking around frantically for the nearest exit).

"What do *I* have to offer? I'm not . . . smart enough . . . brave enough . . . popular enough . . . cute enough . . . (**FILL IN *YOUR* VERY BEST EXCUSE HERE**). And I'm sure not old enough! Why would God want *me* to lead?!"

Good question. Here's an even better one: Why *not* you? After all, who knows you better than God does? Who looks beyond all those "outside" things, and sees into your heart? Who filled you with more gifts and talents than you can possibly imagine? Who planned a special and wonderful purpose for your life long before you were born?

> MATTHEW 6:33: "BUT SEEK FIRST THE KING-DOM OF GOD AND HIS RIGHTEOUSNESS, AND ALL THESE THINGS SHALL BE ADDED TO YOU." (NKJV)

And who but God knows all the wonders you *can* do—if you *choose to do so*?

Quick, Before It's Too Late!

(You're Not Getting Any Younger, You Know!)

And as for not being old enough?

Sorry . . . YOUTH IS NO EXCUTH!

(Come to think of it, aren't *you* the one who usually goes ballistic when someone else starts that "too young" routine?! Hmm?)

Well, someone who will never think you are too young is God!

The fact is that God often chooses young people to do His most important work. Think about a shepherd boy named David, who was the youngest and the "least likely to succeed" of Jesse's sons. David, the one his father didn't even bother to introduce to the prophet Samuel. David, who could barely lift King Saul's sword, or stand up in the royal armor. David, who faced a giant with nothing but a sling in his hand—and God's power in his spirit!

1 SAMUEL 16:7: "GOD DOES NOT SEE THE SAME WAY PEOPLE SEE. PEOPLE LOOK AT THE OUTSIDE OF A PERSON, BUT THE LORD LOOKS AT THE HEART."

Joan of Arc was seventeen when she was called to save a kingdom. A Jewish teenager named Anne Frank touched the conscience of the world with her Holocaust diary. John Wesley, who founded the Methodist Church, and John Calvin, who was a leader in the Protestant Reformation, began their ministries at age seventeen. And Bill Bright's

Campus Crusade for Christ has won more than a billion souls for God.

Too young to be leaders? I don't think so!

Relax, You Don't Have to Change the World!

But you might consider improving your little corner. And by choosing to be a leader at school you can do just that!

MATTHEW 5:14–16:
"YOU ARE THE LIGHT OF THE WORLD ... LET YOUR LIGHT SO SHINE BEFORE MEN, THAT THEY MAY SEE YOUR GOOD WORKS AND GLORIFY YOUR FATHER IN HEAVEN." (NKJV)

Still not convinced? Afraid you don't have the right stuff? Aren't you forgetting something— and Someone? The One who waits with loving patience for the chance to pour out all the riches you could possibly need to fulfill His purpose for your life.

And, of course, once you ask, God always throws in a little "extra." As you work at developing your leadership abilities, you'll find some other pretty amazing things happening.

YOU'LL "GROW" iNTO A stronger, more confident, and **MORE iNTERESTiNG PERSON.** You'll master skills and talents that will last a lifetime, in *everything* you do. You'll taste the joy of actually making a *difference.*

Just Let Your Light Shine!

Best of all, when you become a leader, your Christian walk will take on new power and meaning. You'll be able to influence your classmates and friends for good—sharing your faith, values, and spiritual goals—because you're one of them. You will speak their language.

You can change their lives!

You can show them God, working through you!

Every generation must influence its own generation for Christ. *You* can reach yours . . . striking a spark . . . lighting the fire . . . right at school.

Just the way God planned. Right from the start.

2

What Is This Leadership Thing Anyway? (And What Does It Have to Do with Me?)

Leadership is a fact of life, and it has *everything* to do with you. It's something we all do—even though we don't always know we're doing it.

Don't think so? Can't imagine yourself leading anyone, anywhere? Okay, how about that movie you just *loved*? You know, the one you went on (and on) about, until your friends just *had* to see it, too. Or what about that time you smiled and waved at grumpy old Mr. Adams—and actually got a smile back?!

But those are such little *things*, you're probably thinking. *Anyone can do that.*

Exactly. Anyone.

The truth is that we all lead—or are led— lots of times every day. In things little and big. Usually without even thinking about it. So imagine what you could do if you led *on purpose*, and if you knew the *secret* of leadership . . . influence.

Look behind You. Is Anyone Following?

If someone is, then YOU HAVE INFLUENCE. Something you said, or did, caused someone else to follow along where *you* led. That's what influence is, the ability to get followers.

Anyone who thinks he is leading but has no one following him is only taking a walk.

Without influence, without followers, you can't lead at all. With it . . . ah, *with* it . . .

Everyone Influences Someone

Of course, you do have to be careful, because influence works both ways—for good and for not so good. What if, for instance, that one cigarette you and your friends try "just for fun" turns out to be the start of a really dangerous habit for one of those friends? On the other hand, your steady attendance at church *could* lead a friend closer to God. The truth is that we never know for sure whom we influence, or how much. We just know that it's an awesome responsibility.

> "ONE LIFE STAMPS AND INFLUENCES ANOTHER, WHICH IN TURN STAMPS AND INFLUENCES ANOTHER, ON AND ON, UNTIL THE SOUL OF HUMAN EXPERIENCE BREATHES ON IN GENERATIONS WE'LL NEVER EVEN MEET."
>
> **—MARY KAY BLAKELY,**
> *WAKE ME WHEN IT'S OVER*

Still doubt the power of influence? Just think of the times a person or event touched your life.

Maybe it was a teacher or a coach who believed in you when you didn't believe in yourself. And because that person did, you started believing, too—and amazed yourself!

Maybe it was something like Y2K or the Columbine High School tragedy that changed the way you looked at your safe, predictable world.

Or maybe it was a friend making fun of that favorite old sweater of yours—the one you *never* wore again. Influence. The power to change things. Kind of rearranges the whole idea of leadership, doesn't it?

Will the Real Leader Please Stand Up!

So, who *would* you call a leader? Just check out the Bible, history, or TV for names of people we could all agree are leaders. Jesus, the Son of God, of course. Moses. David. Queen Esther. Martin Luther King, Jr. Columbine martyr Rachel Scott. People whose lives and words and actions changed things for the better. Leaders for sure.

But so is someone like Oprah Winfrey who

influences the way we think about the world. Or what about Michael Jordan? He sells a *lot* of Nikes. Not because he's a shoe expert, but because kids (and grownups) want to be like Michael. He has influence. So do a lot of other sports and entertainment stars. And whether their example is good or bad (and sometimes it's *very* bad), if people admire their talent and want to be like them, they have influence. They are leaders.

Kind of a scary thought, right?

What Kind of Influence Are You Going to Be?

How *are* you going to use your power to change what other people do and think and feel?

Well, of *course* you want to use your influence to lead in ways that make things better and lift people up. Right?

Right??? (Hello? I can't *hear* you. Having a slight case of stage fright?)

That's okay. It's natural to be a little nervous about something you're not sure you know how to do—which is a very good reason to find out more about what makes this leadership thing tick. Because once you know *how* something works, then you can make it work for *you.*

Surprise! You May Already Be a Leader!

Maybe your class or club decides to collect gloves, hats, and socks for a homeless shelter— and you're put in charge of Operation Warmup! It's up to you to see that the right things happen: that word gets out around school, there are places to leave donations, all those socks and gloves are sorted and paired up, someone takes them to the shelter.

> # There's nothing more powerful than an idea whose time has come. (And someone to get the ball rolling!)

So you pick people for each job, make sure they know what they're supposed to do, and check that they're doing it. You also handle any glitches. And, if you're smart, **you say "thanks" and "good job" a lot!**

People follow you because you're the leader—by **position**—for this project. *And only this project!* Don't think so? Just *try* getting your publicity chairman to help with your chores at home!

Then There Are the Leaders Who Are Just ... Well ... Cool!

You know them. Kids who seem to *sail* through life, always in the thick of interesting and exciting things. Kids we *like* being around, because they make us feel good about ourselves.

Want to know their secret?

They really, truly like and care about other people. That's it. And that's *everything*! And it's not something you can fake for long. It has to come from the heart. And when it does, it shows. No wonder they attract followers—in many situations.

He's the one everyone looks at when you're deciding where to go or whom to sit with during lunch break. *She's* the one who can make a club *the* club to join. *They're* the ones whose opinion on just about anything is the opinion that counts! They lead by our permission. And we follow them because we want to.

No way! you may be thinking. *No way I could ever be that cool, have that kind of influence.* Yes, you can. Remember, you know the secret: Lead from the heart, with *real* love and care for others!

Leadership: HEART—'REAL' OR . . . NO DEAL!

But for Real Excitement . . . Make Things Happen!

Here's where the fun really starts. Where a leader—where *you*—can make a *difference* in your school!

"Wait a minute," you might say. "What's wrong with just being cool and having influence with my friends? Sounds pretty good to me."

Really though, how long can you just hang out with friends without everyone, including you, getting a little . . . well . . . bored?! That's when people start to drift away, to follow someone who is *doing* things. You know, the kids who make things *happen* . . . plan that over-the-top successful car wash, pull off that great club party, spearhead a schoolwide Honor Code, get things *done*. This is leadership by PRODUCTION, and it's very exciting to be around—and to *do*.

Think about it. Isn't there at least one thing at school you'd like to change?

Is there a problem with bullying? HOW ARE NEW OR DIFFERENT KIDS TREATED? Could your school be a kinder, friendlier place? And what can *you* do to make that happen? How can you get things started?

You get the idea. And when you're a "happening" kind of leader, you can turn an idea into action!

3
Okay, I'm Leading! (Gulp!) Now What?! (The Fine Art of Getting All Your Ducks in a Row)

So you've decided to take the plunge. Well, come on in—the water's fine!

And don't worry about getting in over your head. You're about to acquire a very handy little "survival" tool: priorities. (Eeuuw!) Sounds pretty "serious" and dull, right? Well, just wait 'til you see what these clever little beauties can help you do—by whatever name you call them.

A Priority by Any Other Name
Is Simply a Goal

And you've always had those. Sure you have. Getting to stay up an extra half-hour when you were just a sprout. Talking Dad into that camping trip. Making it to class on time. Meeting that really cute "somebody." Cleaning your room—although that may be more *Mom's* goal than yours!

The point is that goals are the first step to accomplishment. And when they come along one at a time, things usually work out pretty well. Because you can concentrate all your effort on getting that one thing done. It's when you have more than one thing at a time to achieve—and leaders always do—that life gets . . . complicated.

Unless . . . you have a plan for deciding which "do-me-first" you actually do first! And that's when **priorities** swoop in to *save the day.* Snapping the big picture into focus. Shining the spotlight on what's really important. Helping you decide what's first, what's next, what's left.

Are You Singing the "Too Busy" Blues?

Maybe it's time to change your tune—by calling on your new best friend: **PRIORITIES**. They're also a very powerful self-leadership tool—a reality check to keep your life in balance, and you on track with becoming the kind of person you want to be.

- Priorities help you decide if the goals you're setting in your life are the right goals for you.

- Priorities help you focus on what's really important spiritually.

- Priorities remind you that the very best leadership is the leadership that brings others closer to Jesus.

- Priorities help you make your time, and your life, count.

Putting you in charge—by turning one big, scary job into a lot of smaller "piece of cake" chunks.

So let's hear it for every leader's secret weapon . . .

PRIORITIES . . . GOALS WITH "ATTITUDE"

Juggling 101

So, here you are, costume chairman for your class play. And they're doing (yikes!) *Julius Caesar*! (I know. Weird, huh? But your English teacher *loves* Shakespeare.) Still, how hard could it be? A few sheets for togas, some sandals, a laurel wreath or two . . . and you're home free. Well . . . maybe.

Don't forget, you also have a history test looming on the horizon, music lessons, church youth group, *and* chores at home. You want to do a good job on all of it. And you especially don't want to let the kids in the play down.

So you *set some goals*—which usually begin with questions:

☐ How can I do the best job in the least amount of time?

- ☐ What does the director expect from me?
- ☐ Who's going to help? (Does my committee come with "warm bodies," or do *I* have to find them?)
- ☐ What about those "easy" sheets? (Is there a budget to buy them, or do we beg, borrow, and scrounge?)
- ☐ And, come to think of it, how *do* you drape a toga?

Then (if you haven't totally freaked out by now) you take a deep breath and remind yourself of something very important: **It's not how hard you work, it's how smart you work!**

Place Your Order, Please!

And you are going to work very smartly indeed. Because the next thing you do is **prioritize your goals**—put things in order of importance. And (surprise!) it's not all that hard to do. You've already listed everything that *has* to happen. Now you simply ask yourself: What

Time is God's precious gift to you. How you use your time is your gift back to God.

has to happen *before* something else can happen? See, things are starting to line up!

(By the way, this is the perfect stage to get those other "warm bodies" involved, because people who get to help decide what's going to happen are a lot more excited about making it happen!)

Then, with priorities neatly in line—and your committee organized and ready to go— you lead in one of the most important ways of all. You make sure you *all* resist the temptation to "talk it to death," and, instead, jump right in and . . . do it! In other words—(*and* in the language of Caesar's time)—you . . .

CARPE DIEM!
(No, not "seize the fish"!)
SEIZE THE DAY!

Next thing you know (ta dah!) you've gone from "What are we supposed to *do*?" to Julius & Company stepping onstage in perfectly draped togas, every laurel wreath neatly in place. (Go ahead, take your bow! But don't forget to share the applause with your hard-working committee.)

ECCLESIASTES 3:1: TO EVERYTHING THERE IS A SEASON, A TIME FOR EVERY PURPOSE UNDER HEAVEN. (NKJV)

Fun, isn't it? Making things happen. And once you've shown you *can*— and that you know how to make it *fun* for everyone involved—you'll get plenty of chances to do it again.

And again. And again. So many chances, in fact, that you're suddenly face-to-face with another

VIQ

(Very Important Question).

Help! Am I Trying to Do Too Much?

It can happen. One of the sneaky little pitfalls of leadership is the temptation to spread yourself too thin. You say "yes" to everything. And before long you're so involved in so much that other important areas of your life get cheated. Are you allowed to say "no"? Yes, you are!

THE FACT IS: YOU CAN'T DO IT ALL.

THE GOOD NEWS IS: YOU DON'T HAVE TO.

THE TRICK IS: DOING WHAT *YOU* DO BEST!

4

If You "Talk the Talk," Ya Gotta "Walk the Walk"! (In Other Words ... Get Real!)

Okay, you've stuck in a toe, tested the waters, maybe even made a modest splash or two. And you've decided you kind of like this leadership thing. After all, what's *not* to like? You've had fun with old friends, made some new ones, and helped make good stuff happen. And it *is* pretty neat, having people starting to look to you for answers and ideas.

MATTHEW 7:12:
"THERE-FORE, WHAT-EVER YOU WANT MEN TO DO TO YOU, DO ALSO TO THEM." (NKJV)

Reality check! If you want to make sure all of the above keeps on happening ...

Will the Real You Please Stand Up!

The "real" me??? What does *that* mean?!

Glad you asked. Because we've just bumped headlong into the A-#1, absolutely essential, gotta-have-it, won't-last-long-without-it, ingredient of leadership: Integrity!

Oh, no, not *another* of those serious words! Not to worry, you're going to love what integrity does for you.

GOTTA BE ME? JUST TURN THE INTEGRITY KEY!

INTEGRITY SETS YOU FREE, to be . . . yourself! Of course, you may still be figuring out just *who* that is. But with integrity in your corner you don't have to pretend to be anything other than the very best custom-designed-by-God *you* that you can be, right at this moment!

With integrity, all the pieces fit. Nothing about you "argues" with anything else. What you say is what you do. Your promise is some-

> "To thine own self be true, and it must follow, as the night the day, thou canst not then be false to any man."
>
> —Hamlet I, iii, 75

thing people can count on. **Your word is good!**

People trust you—because they know what to expect from you. You're true to yourself, so they feel comfortable that you'll be true to them, too. And who wouldn't want to follow a leader like that?

But **FOLLOW YOU WHERE?** Ah, that *is* the question. Especially since you may not even be sure you've really got your arms around the whole idea of integrity. But we can fix that.

It's Really a Matter of Honor

Honor? Absolutely! Honor is integrity's *other* face. And, no, it didn't ride off into the sunset with the last of the Knights of the Round Table. Honor is alive and well, and still rides to the rescue . . . slays "dragons" . . . saves the day!

Honor is the sword and shield that let you stand tall—and make the tough choices. With honor (integrity) you can let your principles and values show. With honor, you can stand up for what you believe— even when it's not the popular choice. With honor, you can take the lead in doing what you *know* is right.

"THE FIRST KEY TO GREATNESS IS TO BE IN REALITY WHAT WE APPEAR TO BE."

—SOCRATES,
GREEK PHILOSOPHER
AND TEACHER

Honor is real. And, with it, so are *you*. And the "real you" has work to do.

Caution: Watch Out for Slings and Arrows!

Oddly enough, some of the toughest battles-of-honor you'll fight will be *inside* yourself. Don't think so? See if any of this sounds familiar . . .

After all, there really *wasn't* time to study for that test—what with all those school activities you've jumped into. And you really *are* good at math. So what could it hurt if—just this once—you just happened, accidentally, of course, to glance over at your math-whiz buddy Jake's test paper? Hmm? After all, it's not like you don't usually know this stuff cold.

PROVERBS 23:7: "FOR AS HE THINKS IN HIS HEART, SO IS HE." (NKJV)

Sure, keeping a friend's secret *is* important. And you're usually brilliant at keeping your lip zipped. But what Lisa told you at lunch was just *too* delicious not to share! How could it possibly be *your* fault that it's all over school, and Lisa's embarrassed? You only told *one* person—in strictest confidence. Lisa probably told more people than that herself!

HONOR ALERT!!! WHATEVER YOU DO, MAKE SURE IT'S NOT YOU THAT'S FOOLING YOU!

Hey, we never said this honor/integrity thing was *easy*! Just very, very worthwhile. The truth is, you have to keep an eye on yourself pretty much all the time. Before long, though, you're really going to start liking what you see. And because you do, you'll find you're a lot braver than you thought when it comes to working on things *outside* yourself, too.

Just Show Me to the Nearest Dragon!

A smart leader chooses the battle—and the moment. Maybe it's something like smoking or drugs. Well, naturally, you speak up loud and clear about where you stand on *that*. More often, though, you'll find yourself leading in the most powerful way of all—not by what you say, but by what you *do*.

And by the dragons you choose—not all of which are huge, fire-breathing monsters!

Some **DRAGONS ARE NASTY** *little* beasts that sneak up on you when you least expect it.

And, sorry, "ignore it and maybe it'll go away" just doesn't work with these guys. Sooner or later, you'll have to grab that dragon by the tail. Need a for-instance?

Okay, let's take a look around. School pretty

much works for you, right? Most of the time, it's a fun, exciting place (assuming your homework's done, that is). You've got friends. You're comfortable. You belong.

But did you ever wonder what it's like for the kids who are new . . . or different? You know who I mean—the ones who don't "fit in." Their clothes aren't quite right. Or they try *too* hard to be funny, or cool. Some are so shy you can't get a word out of them. Others are noisy, pushy, and really . . . annoying.

Does that mean it's okay to just take the path of least resistance? Go with the flow? Pretend they're not there at all? Maybe even laugh when your friends make fun of them?

HONOR ALERT!!! WHAT GOES AROUND, COMES AROUND!

Or . . . do you listen to that little voice inside? You know, the one that asks you how you'd feel if that were *you* being ignored, put down, or made fun of?

Oh.

Oh, indeed. And there you are: smack-dab up against what philosophers call a "moment of truth." What your friends might call weird. And what honor calls **doing the right thing**.

So you take a deep breath and . . . do it. You invite that new girl with the funny clothes to join you—and your friends—at your lunch table. You find a smile, a friendly word, for that loudmouthed, bragging boy who works so hard for attention. And instead of laughing at unkind remarks, you look your friends in the eye and say—with a smile: "Hey, guys, lets cut 'em a little slack!" And mean it.

So what happens then? Try it and find out.

Integrity is who you are when no one is looking!

You may be very surprised. Because people do what people see! You might even start a trend.

A Legend in Your Own Time?

Maybe. Maybe not. Doesn't matter. Because you're not doing this so other people will like and admire you. You're doing it so *you* will like and admire you! And because you do—because you truly "practice what

"ALWAYS DO RIGHT. THAT WILL GRATIFY SOME PEOPLE AND ASTONISH THE REST."

—MARK TWAIN, AMERICAN HUMORIST AND AUTHOR

you preach"—you'll find yourself leading by example. Although what it really is, is just doing the right thing. (Let the chips—and dragons—fall where they may!)

5

Designing and Building the "New, Improved" You (The Ultimate Do-It-Yourself Project!)

A nip here. A tuck there. A little attitude adjustment. And—*voila!*—the you you've always wanted to be! Of course, change, particularly big change, isn't quite that easy in real life. But there are times—some you choose, some you don't—when change *is* totally—

"Hey."

—necessary. So the best thing to do is—

"HEY!"

Oh, sorry, did you want to say something?

"NOW

WAIT JUST A MINUTE HERE!!!

"You said I should be myself. Now all of a sudden you want me to change?!"

Oops! Sorry again, thought you knew: Change is a fact of life. *Nothing* ever just stays the same. That's not the way God planned things. He didn't shape Creation, shrink-wrap it in plastic, and say, "There! *That's* done." No, instead, He set a universe of infinite possibility in motion. And motion means . . . change!

> "ALL THE FLOWERS OF ALL THE TOMOR-ROWS ARE IN THE SEEDS OF TODAY."
> —CHINESE PROVERB

"But I Like Things Just the Way They Are, Thankyouverymuch!"

Well, of course, you do. Because you don't know what *else* is waiting just around the corner.

Actually, resisting change is not all that unusual. In fact, getting people to go along with change is the toughest challenge a leader faces, because change involves a big leap into the unknown. A leap of faith, you might say, because we don't know what's out there!

For that matter, it's very possible that caterpillars *dread* the thought of becoming butterflies.

"THE UNIVERSE IS CHANGE; OUR LIFE IS WHAT OUR THOUGHTS MAKE IT."

—MARCUS AURELIUS ANTONIUS, ROMAN EMPEROR AND PHILOSOPHER, *MEDITATIONS*

"WINGS?! WHAT IN HEAVEN'S NAME AM I SUPPOSED TO DO WITH THOSE?!"

But, ready or not, change happens. Did you know that your entire body changes—replacing every last cell of you—every seven years? The fact is, you change every day. Your socks. Your mind. Your taste in music. Your attitude. You change because you have to . . . because you want to . . . because you choose to. Without change, nothing grows. Including you.

Face it, there's no escape. So what's it going to be? Going gracefully with the flow, or . . .

Kicking and Screaming All the Way!

You *could* make it tough on yourself—*and* everyone around you. But why would you want to? Some changes are going to happen whether you agree or not. That's a done deal. So the trick is . . . making the change work *for* you. And that begins with changing one other thing first. Your attitude. (Is there no *end* to this change business?!)

> PSALMS 24:1; 27:1: "THE EARTH IS THE LORD'S, AND ALL ITS FULLNESS, THE WORLD AND THOSE WHO DWELL THEREIN . . . THE LORD IS THE STRENGTH OF MY LIFE; OF WHOM SHALL I BE AFRAID?" (NKJV)

Maybe it's the coming move up to high school that has your nerves frazzled. Even worse, new school district lines mean that you—but not most of your friends—are assigned to the new high school clear across town! How on earth can you possibly survive?! Well, you could start with a look at exactly *why* this all is such a disaster.

First of all, it's not *your* idea, which is one of the main reasons people resist change. So the whole thing is going to take some getting used to. And you have no idea what your new school is going to be like, or where anything *is*, or how things *work*. (Oh, no! It's the dreaded "unknown"!) All the places you love going, the things you love doing, will change. (And it's such a cozy, comfortable, familiar little rut!)

Worst of all, you'll be leaving a lot of your friends behind. (No way around it, that *is* a tough one. Good friends *are* irreplaceable.)

By this time there's not a dry eye in the house—especially yours. And that's perfectly natural. It's also a very good time to

TURN THINGS AROUND . . . SEE WHAT'S ON THE OTHER SIDE!

A Little Polish, a Little Faith, and Eureka! . . . a Silver Lining!

See, you *do* have a choice. You can weep and moan, snap at your mom, make everyone around you absolutely miserable because **YOUR LIFE IS RUINED!** Or . . .

You could pull up your socks, get a grip, and think of the whole thing as an adventure. A chance to stretch and grow.

Haven't you always wanted to be more grown-up? Here's your chance.

You made a place for yourself in one school. Why not another? And your new school is going to have clubs to join and things to do, too. Probably some you've never had a chance to try—until now.

But what about your friends-since-kindergarten? How can you leave *them*? Well, you're not exactly dropping off the face of the earth. There are things like telephones, e-mail . . . the mall. Your friends won't be really gone, you know, just out of sight. So you keep in touch and keep those old friends close in your heart. And you *open* your heart to making some pretty neat *new* friends, too.

And when the dreary "What ifs" come calling—**What if I can't cut it? What if nobody likes me? What if I end up alone?**—you look them firmly in the eye, and show them the door. Because you know there's one friend who's *always* with you, and no matter how "strange" the land you find yourself in, He holds it *all* safe in loving hands.

So you take a deep breath, and do what every good leader must be able to do—you not only accept change, you celebrate it! Because standing arm in arm with change is someone you're going to love meeting. The newest, just-released, megapowered version of a very interesting . . . *you*!

6

Taming the Dreaded "Uh-Oh!'s" and "Oh, My!'s" (Problem Can Be Just Another Name for Opportunity)

Your team came up with the best idea in class. (Way to go!) Then it was judged winning project proposal in your grade level. (Outstanding!) And now your group's absolutely brilliant, stroke-of-genius plan is going to represent your entire school at the state science fair! (**Yes!**) As soon, that is, as you all actually *build* the thing.

Piece of cake, right? It *is* a fantastic idea. The science is solid. And some of the best brains in school are working with you.

So what could possibly go wrong?

Well . . . Kevin's wiring plan may need a little work. (Oops!)

Jake's got the flu, so you're short-handed. Karen and Emma can't seem to agree on whether the bubbles should come before, or after, the pendulum begins to swing.

(Oh, my!)
And who'd **have** thought a simple little static

generator **would** cost quite so much! (Uh-oh!)
Welc**ome** to the **real** world which comes **complete**
with **an** occasional
PR o B L E M !

And guess what *that* means?

Hey, Why Is Everyone Looking at Me!

Because you're the team leader—which *also* makes you **vice president in charge of disasters.**

(What, you mean nobody told you?) Wait, come back here! That was the bad news. Here's the good news: **Problem-solving,** one of the biggest challenges of leadership, also offers its greatest opportunities.

> "LITTLE MINDS ARE TAMED AND SUBDUED BY MISFORTUNE, BUT GREAT MINDS RISE ABOVE IT."
>
> —WASHINGTON IRVING, AMERICAN AUTHOR

It's **your chance to shine!** *And* build a terrific reputation as a great leader. Why? Because people don't like problems and will do almost anything to get away from them. In fact . . .

PEOPLE HATE PROBLEMS, AND LOVE PROBLEM-SOLVERS!

Learn to deal cheerfully with glitches, foul-ups, and the occasional catastrophe, and you'll have people lining up to follow you. You'll also pick up some very useful talents that spill over into everything else you do in life. And who *wouldn't* want to be incredibly flexible, resourceful, and light of foot?

Problems Can Trip You Up . . . or Teach You to Be Nimble!

Why not just jump right in and give it a whirl? Problem-solving—like every other leadership skill—is something you can learn. All it takes is the right attitude, and the right action plan.

The first thing to come to grips with is the fact that a problem is not the universe picking on *you*. A lot of things happen that are outside your control. It's how you deal with them that makes the difference. To put it another way . . .

THE PROBLEM ISN'T THE PROBLEM. IT'S HOW YOU REACT TO THE PROBLEM!

In fact, it's problems (and the ways we deal with them) that give meaning to life. An eagle has to struggle mightily to beat his wings against the wind. Yet it's the wind that lifts him up. Some of the most hopeful, joyful psalms were born in difficulty. And most of the Epistles that set our spirits free were written in prisons.

What counts, you see, isn't the size of the problem . . . but the size of the inner person. Life is full of opportunities to grumble about lemons . . . or make lemonade! Your choice.

Tiptoe through Your "Garden"!

The first tiny shoots of trouble can crop up almost overnight. A smart leader pays attention, learns to recognize potential problems, and nips them in the bud before a small glitch grows into a big emergency. How will you know? If you're watching, and listening, you will. And you'll have a plan.

"PLAN? WHAT PLAN?! I DON'T HAVE A PLAN!!!"

Relax, you have one now. A plan *and* a secret weapon: your common sense. That's what problem-solving really is, plain old common sense—with (okay) a dash of strategy. A healthy survival instinct doesn't hurt, either. Stir briskly, and you're ready to whip up a solution.

" ... if you want the rainbow, you gotta put up with the rain."

—Dolly Parton

Catch the Rhythm

Every project has one. And a smart leader stays tuned in to that rhythm—its ups and downs, its rough and smooth spots—*everything*. What your team is up to. Where things are headed. Who's happy, who's not. In fact, once you grow your leadership "antenna," you'll sense when something isn't right. IDENTIFY THE PROBLEM (or problem-to-be) before things get out of hand. Jake's flu. The Great Karen and Emma Bubble Debate. That not-quite-right wiring plan. The skyrocketing cost of static generators. You'd be wise to do something about all these things now! But which one do you tackle first? Good question. And a good time to . . .

Watch Your Step!

You may be good, but there's a limit to the number of things even *you* can do at one time. So you call on another leadership skill you've been mastering. You PRIORITIZE THE PROBLEM—putting the most serious threat at the top of your "to do" list. Then you work your way down the list, lining them *all* up in order of importance— from power for your project to Jake's flu. And you're on your way to a solution. Hold it! You're not there yet. There's one more thing you need. Information. Details. The real scoop. Because it's information that lets you . . .

PSALM 46:1: GOD IS OUR REFUGE AND STRENGTH, A VERY PRESENT HELP IN TROUBLE. (NKJV)

Pick Up the Pace

You can't fix it if you don't know where—or if—it's "broke." So you take a closer look, and **define the problem.** Ask questions. Get the facts. Talk to the people who know.

- *Can* Kevin fix his wiring plan, and how long will it take?
- *Will* Karen and Emma work things out on their own, as they usually do? Or does this bubble thing need a referee?
- *How* can you get your hands on a static generator you can't afford? Is there something else you could use instead? Can you borrow one?
- *Does* Jake know when he'll be back in action? Can he suggest someone to fill in for him until he is?

All stuff you need to know. All stuff you do know now. Which takes you directly to the fun part . . .

Jump Right in and Fix It!

Now—information in hand and team involved—you all proceed directly to where you've been headed all along: solutions!

Go ahead, strut your stuff a little. You've earned it. You've stretched yourself in new and important ways. You've *used* the talents and skills God gave you. You've walked in His ways, and you've moved a little closer to becoming everything He intends you to be.

"DIFFICULTIES ARE GOD'S ERRAND'S. AND WHEN WE ARE SENT UPON THEM, WE SHOULD ESTEEM IT A PROOF OF GOD'S CONFIDENCE."

—HENRY WARD BEECHER, PROTESTANT PREACHER NOTED FOR HIS ELOQUENCE

7

Enclosed: Everything You Need to Succeed (Batteries Not Included!)

It's true. God sends you into life—prepackaged and ready-to-assemble—with more talents and gifts than any reasonable person could possibly expect.

But what you do with His gifts, how you use your amazing talents, what you make of your incredible possibilities—well, that's entirely up to you.

Through His gift of free will, God puts *you* in charge. He trusts you to provide the energy—the battery—that makes His purpose for your life *work*. Which means . . .

GUESS "WATT"?
YOU ARE THE "BATTERY"!

Wow! Pretty big responsibility, isn't it? (Electrifying, you could even say.) And more than a little scary. Until you remember that you already have everything you need to put together the life—the *person*—God always intended. He's done His part. As for the rest, well, THAT'S YOUR JOB. And it's all a matter of . . . attitude.

Yup. Attitude. Your own special point of view that controls *how* you see the world and

Misery is an option. So is joy!

what you make of each day. It's the difference between up or down, a smile or a frown, the feel-goods or the blahs. Attitude. And it's all up to you because—and here's the really neat thing about attitude—you get to *choose* it!

Really. You get to decide—in fact, you *must* decide—how you're going to take on each day, how you're going to make "your light shine"!

Shining Beacon . . . or Dim Bulb?

Which would you rather be? That's kind of a no-brainer, right? Who wouldn't want to draw people to them, *and* make them glad they came?! Well, that's attitude at work.

Your attitude not only *tells* people a lot about you, it affects how they *feel* about you. It can be a powerful attraction, or a mega-turnoff. Bring people close, or make them want to run as fast as they can in the opposite direction (which can make leadership a trifle difficult). It can be your strongest asset—as a leader and as a person— or your biggest drawback.

In fact, attitude is so powerful, it really should come with a warning label:

HANDLE WITH CARE: ATTITUDE IS HIGHLY CONTAGIOUS!

Don't think so? Try this. Name three people—kids or grownups—you know whom you especially admire. People you love to spend time with, wish you were like. Now ask yourself how you would describe each of them to a total stranger. Well, surprise, surprise! It isn't how they look, or how smart or talented they are that comes to mind first, is it? It's how it feels to be around them—how they make everything, including you, seem a little brighter, a little more fun, a little more hopeful.

PSALM 118:24: THIS IS THE DAY THE LORD HAS MADE; WE WILL REJOICE AND BE GLAD IN IT. (NKJV)

We like being around people like this because their positive outlook—their attitude—just kind of rubs off on us, too. They "broadcast" energy and joy.

Like to have some of that power for your very own? You can—with a little work.

You, Too, Can Send Off Sparks!

Of course, your attitude power might need a slight tune-up first. Never hurts to check and see what kind of signals you're sending out to the world.

For starters, are you a happy person? No, you don't have to walk around grinning madly all the time! In fact, people might start to wonder about you if you did. But, basically—an occasional down day aside—does life feel good to you? Can you cope with most of what comes your way without getting *too* bent out of shape?

Speaking of which, what *does* drive you nuts? Is it certain people—parents, friends, that annoying kid in history class? Or is it situations, stuff that happens that you can—or can't—control?

Most important (and this *is* the biggie), how do you handle what's bugging you? Because sooner or later, you will have to handle it—*and* your attitude. There's no escape . . .

YOU CAN RUN, BUT YOU CAN'T HIDE. ATTITUDE CATCHES UP WITH YOU EVERY TIME!

Okay, so you're *not* perfect. The question is: What are you going to do about it? How are you going to get that attitude of yours humming along on all eight cylinders? Well, you could start with a role model—a *perfect* role model: Jesus, the Son of God.

Throwing the Switch from Negative to Positive

So how *do* you become the kind of person—the kind of leader—who inspires the *best* in all concerned? How *do* you make sure "whassup" is you—and everyone around you?

You've already begun. Remember those questions you asked yourself about how you react to life and problems and people? Well, your answers are your blueprint for change.

The Ultimate Attitude Power Source

Jesus lived the perfect example of Christian attitude. His every word, thought, and action was directed by love! He looked at what mankind was . . . and saw what mankind could be. Then He showed us—down to the very last breath of life—what love can do.

He was filled with infinite compassion and patience, but He never wavered from truth. He understood our struggles and shortcomings, but He insisted we be everything His Father in heaven intended us to be. Because He knows we can be that . . . when we begin with love.

Want to work on your attitude? Jesus gave you the key. All you have to do is turn it.

(See, you're halfway there already!)

Now you make a positive effort to change the feelings and actions that need work. And that begins with right thinking. Changing your mind-set! Because that's where *all* change starts.

As a very wise man once said:

COGITO ERGO SUM. HUH? SAY WHAT?!?

(Okay, so this very wise man insisted on saying it in Latin. Sort of a personal quirk of his.) But in Latin, or English, what it says is, "I think, therefore I am." And he was absolutely right. What happens in our minds is what happens in our lives. Our feelings come from our thoughts! And when you change your thoughts, you control those feelings that have been messing you up. You change your vision of the world, and your place in it.

If at First You Don't Succeed . . .

Give yourself a break! Sure, you keep on trying. But you also remember that this is all supposed to be fun. You'll get there, and you'll enjoy the trip a lot more if you're smiling most of the way. In fact, it would be downright ungrateful to the One who planned the journey *not* to smile.

Life is a gift. And your best thank-you to the Giver is to throw your arms around every day . . . and fill it with joy.

Look Out, World, Here You Come!

Plans work, if you work.

So take your pen and write. (Write?!) You bet. Ink on paper makes it all real. Write down the right thinking in the situations you want to change.

☐ Are you impatient with people who don't think or act as quickly as you do?

    Write: Patience with others.

☐ Do you fly off the handle when someone disagrees with you?

    Write: Tolerance for other points of view.

☐ Do you get frustrated when things don't go your way?

    Write: Persistence.

☐ Do you worry too much about what people think of you?

    Write: Trust in myself and God. And underline it!

Then practice, practice, practice. (That is how you get to Carnegie Hall, you know.) Put yourself in at least one of these situations every day. But this time watch yourself try really hard to handle it in a different way. In fact, ask someone else—a trusted friend, a brother or sister, a favorite teacher—to watch, too. And to tell you how you're doing.

8

Having Your Cake and Eating It, Too (The Delicious Benefits of Sharing!)

Well, no *wonder* you're excited. Your award-winning school chorus has been invited to sing at the White House! You're going to descend—the entire unruly, but very talented, lot of you—on Washington, D.C. You'll have a great time! There's so much to see and do. The White House, the Capitol, the National Zoo . . . and you could spend a whole glorious day at the museums of the Smithsonian Institution. Trust me, you'll freak out over the Smithsonian collections. They're filled with more strange and wonderful—sometimes unbelievable—"stuff" than you can possibly imagine.

So when do you leave?

Oh.

Yes, figuring out how to pay for the group trip *is* a slight hitch. Guess you're all going to have to "sing for your supper." (Can you spell f-u-n-d–r-a-i-s-i-n-g?) A lot of somebodies are going to have to sell a lot of somethings to cover chorus expenses. *A lot.* Well, good luck to the chairman of *that* committee!

What? Oh, that would be . . . *you.* Elected? Appointed? Shanghaied? Not that it matters. The job is yours. The entire chorus is counting on you. And you've got a lot of ground to cover between now and D.C. *A lot.*

Which certainly explains why you're perched on the edge of your seat, lacing up your running shoes. Looking just a tad . . . nervous? Never mind, you can do a brilliant job. If you start off on the right foot, that is, and get that all-important *first* step right.

But don't let me keep you. In fact, I'll hold the door for you. Good luck!

Oh, just one more thing before you go—no,

Nobody cares how much you know, 'til they know how much you care.

don't worry about the chair, I'll pick it up—you *do* know what that first step *is,* don't you?

On second thought, maybe we *should* talk a little more. How 'bout over lunch? Just think of it as a little food for thought.

Please Pass the Carrots

How you treat people—the kind of relationships you build—is the truest measure of genuine leadership and the surest way to influence people in *all* the ways that count.

So how *do* you build great relationships—

A Heaping Helping of Humble Pie

Want to be a really great leader? Then get ready to swallow a little pride. Because until you do, you can't take that oh-so-important first step to success—putting the spotlight on others! Which is truly where it belongs, as every smart cookie of a leader knows. Not that your role isn't important. In fact, they can't do it without you (or someone like you). On the other hand, you can't do it without them, either!

So you sweeten the deal for the kids you're counting on, by letting them know how important they are—to the project and to you—right from the get-go. No matter how outstanding your plans or ideas are, there just isn't a better way to get everything—and everyone—off to a flying start.

create a crew of "happy campers" eager to go where you want them to go? Well, here's a little tip you might want to keep top-of-mind. It's something well known to anyone who has ever tried to get a stubborn mule to go in a certain direction.

A CARROT BEATS A STICK EVERY TIME!

If you're in a formal state of mind, you can call it by its proper name: **motivation**. That, by any name, is simply the art of showing people *why* they want to go where—by an amazing coincidence—you want them to go. You keep the reward (the Washington, D.C., trip) front and center every time you talk about the work (they will actually go out and sell the somethings).

And speaking of the somethings, what exactly *is* it you're all going to peddle so persuasively? Here's another great opportunity to involve everyone in the process. How? Ask them. Then listen, **really listen**, to the answers. You'll be amazed at all the creative ideas that come flying back. And you'll say so, loud and clear!

Suddenly, *your* job is a lot easier. And everyone

is a lot happier. After all, who doesn't like to feel worthwhile and important? And be told so—at frequent intervals!

A LITTLE APPRECIATION IS GOOD. A LOT IS GREAT!

(No, you won't spoil them, you'll just make them want more.)

Heavy on the Honey, Hold the Vinegar!

Whether it's flies or followers you're out to catch, a little "sweet" will take you a lot farther than all the "sour" in the world. Something else to remember: You dish out one or the other just about every time you open your mouth!

Words have power, especially yours as leader. They can also be pretty painful to swallow. So you use them wisely—and kindly. To encourage and uplift. To bring out the *best* in others, and yourself. And you never—ever—use them to hurt. Because hurt, they can.

STICKS AND STONES ONLY BREAK BONES; WORDS STRIKE TO THE HEART!

But where do you find the *right* words? In a very unexpected place: the actions—and reactions—of other people. In short, before you speak, you *listen*! And you listen with more than your ears. Your ears will catch only what people *say*. It's what they *do* that clues you in to what they want—and need—to hear from you.

You listen with your *heart* . . . then you lead from the same place.

> GALATIANS 5:13–14: . . . "THROUGH LOVE SERVE ONE ANOTHER. FOR ALL THE LAW IS FULFILLED IN ONE WORD, EVEN IN THIS: 'YOU SHALL LOVE YOUR NEIGHBOR AS YOURSELF.'" (NKJV)

Serve It Up with Love

One of the greatest gifts of leadership is the opportunity to see people in a new light—think about them in a new way.

Leading from the heart opens you up to the wonderful possibilities tucked away inside "ordinary" kids. It makes you more sensitive to the ways we're all the same. And reminds you that differences aren't something to be afraid of, but something to celebrate!

"DO ORDINARY THINGS WITH EXTRAORDINARY LOVE."
—MOTHER TERESA

Best of all, you learn how to put yourself in another's place. Because that's where you need to go to truly understand what he needs from you. And once you're there, you're face-to-face with an amazing reality. No matter how neat, weird, cool, or different they are on the outside, *inside* they're just like you! And helping them do—and be—their best is the very same thing as helping yourself.

How can you help but love 'em?! *And* let it show? And because you do, because love is a powerful magnet, something awesome happens. A collection of separate individuals— each with his or her own ideas, agendas, and hang-ups—comes together as a unified *team* with one powerful purpose.

And the rest is history.

Enjoy Your Just Desserts

The taste of success is all the sweeter when it's shared. And—together—you *and* your team (your very large, enthusiastic, involved—and appreciated—team) have pulled off a pretty amazing feat. You've sold more "stuff" to more people—and had more fun doing it—than any chorus ever!

No wonder you're all grinning your way through the Smithsonian!

Enjoy.

"SHE DID NOT TALK TO PEOPLE AS IF THEY WERE STRANGE HARD SHELLS SHE HAD TO CRACK TO GET INSIDE. SHE TALKED AS IF SHE WERE ALREADY IN THE SHELL. IN THEIR VERY SHELL."

—MARITA BONNER, WRITER, FROM "NOTHING NEW" IN *FRYE STREET AND ENVIRONS*

9

The Care and Feeding of Dreams (What You See Is What You Get!)

You've probably heard *this* a gazillion or two times: Stop **daydreaming!** But, you know, that's not necessarily an *all*-occasion piece of good advice.

Well, sure, you should choose your moments—which do *not* include the middle of math class, a lecture from your dad, or while baby-sitting your little brother. But there are times when daydreams are not only highly recommended, they are absolutely essential!

What is a daydream, after all, but **your mind**

flying free, playing with lovely possibilities that seem out of reach in the real world? It's you, talking to yourself about what you'd *like* to happen. It's the you-who-could-be creating a **vision** of what *might* be!

STOP DAYDREAMING? NO WAY! Throw your arms around your dreams and hold them tight. Because it's dreams that show you the most important part of any journey: your destination. After all . . .

YOU CAN'T GET TO THE MALL 'TIL YOU KNOW WHERE THE MALL IS!

Life is full of goodies, too. Learn to harness your dreams, and you're almost there.

Dream Wrangling Made Easy . . . Sort Of

Of course, there are dreams and . . . dreams. (That one about you performing onstage with your favorite rock star, for instance? In two words: Im-Possible!) But your dream—your vision—about what you want to *be*, what you want to *do* next week . . . next year . . . out in the world? Well, that can change your life. And that's worth more than a little effort.

Uh-oh. Just as you suspected, this dream business is going to take work. But then, doesn't anything worth having take work? You already know how to dream. Creating dreams and visions that *work* is only a step away. All you have to do is . . .

ISAIAH 40:31: . . . THOSE WHO WAIT ON THE LORD SHALL RENEW THEIR STRENGTH; THEY SHALL MOUNT UP WITH WINGS LIKE EAGLES . . . (NKJV)

Look Inside Yourself. What in your life doesn't feel "right"? What would you like to change? What have you always wanted—but didn't have the nerve—to try?

Look Behind You. What mistakes have you made? What did they teach you? What have you always been afraid of?

Look Around You. What needs doing? How do people see you? What do you *wish* they saw?

Look Ahead. Where do you see yourself in

ten years? In twenty? What difference would you like to make in the world?

Look Above. What does God expect of you? What special gifts has He given you? Are you using them?

Now pick just one thing (starting small is always a good idea) and—in your head—change it. Paint a *new* picture, one that shows things the way you want them to be. Then paint yourself into the picture, too, front and center. Now stand back and admire your vision. *Every day*! And you know what?

> "ALL OUR DREAMS CAN COME TRUE, IF WE HAVE THE COURAGE TO PURSUE THEM."
>
> —WALT DISNEY, INVENTOR, DREAMER, FILMMAKER, AND FOUNDER OF THE DISNEY THEME PARKS

The more you look at your new "picture," the more real it becomes. And the more you'll find yourself looking for ways to make it happen!

As a matter of fact, *now* would be a great time to think about your personal goal for the future. Is college in the picture? Do you want to be a doctor . . . a Web designer . . . a pilot . . . or (fill in your dream goal here)? Or maybe you have no idea. Well, now's a great time to start planning—*and* working on your special vision.

LIKING WHAT YOU'RE SEEING IS THE FIRST STEP TO BE-ING!

Hanging In and Hanging On!

By the way, when you're packing for the "trip" to your wonderful future, be sure to toss in a little patience. The truth is that dreams take time. But if you stick with them, they'll stick with you.

And you can for sure count on some bumps in the road . . . maybe even a mountain or two to move on the way to your dream. Lucky you! Believe it or not, those challenges and obstacles may be your best friends, because they teach you how to grit your teeth and hang in, *to trust your dreams,* to keep hope alive.

> LUKE 12:48: "FOR EVERYONE TO WHOM MUCH IS GIVEN, FROM HIM MUCH WILL BE REQUIRED . . ." (NKJV)

They teach you something else, too—the irresistible power of dreams to find a way around . . . through . . . or *over* every mountain. Because every dream comes equipped with something you may never have thought you'd have . . .

WHEN LIFE RAISES UP MOUNTAINS, DREAMS GIVE YOU WINGS!

Always Save Room for "Bumblebee" Dreams!

Bumblebee dreams?! Oh yes, they're the very best kind. Because those are the dreams that come once you decide "impossible" is only a word in the dictionary. The dreams that begin every time you look at a beautiful possibility and say, "Why not . . . ?"

> "YOU SEE THINGS; AND YOU SAY, 'WHY?' BUT I DREAM THINGS THAT NEVER WERE; AND I SAY, 'WHY NOT?' "
>
> —G. B. SHAW, IRISH-BORN DRAMATIST, CRITIC, AND ESSAYIST

Think about it for a minute. What do you suppose bumblebees might dream? Could it be that they can fly?

Because they really shouldn't be able to, you know. Absolutely impossible. No way. Just can't happen. From an engineering standpoint, this fuzzy little buzzer is an aeronautical disaster. That chunky, awkward body is just way too heavy for those tiny little wings to lift. A lot of people will tell you: design-wise, bumblebees can't fly.

The thing is, **no one tells the bumblebee.** So he flies anyway. Maybe because he thinks he can. Something inside says "up" is where he needs to be. So he does what it takes to get there. He works extra hard to overcome what holds him down—from gravity to what people think.

His fragile little wings pump furiously into a blur of energy. That chubby little body starts feeling not quite so heavy, the odds against flying not quite so strong. He pumps his wings even harder. He finds strength he didn't know he had. The sky calls his name. And he flies!

With the right dreams, so can you!

10

Stalking the Wild Promise (The Art of Turning Dreams into Reality)

Your dream—your vision—is a beautiful thing, wild and free. Be careful it doesn't get away from you!

Right now that fine-feathered dream of yours is really nothing more—and nothing less—than a PROMISE. A promise you make to yourself! And until someone makes that promise come true, that's all it will *ever* be.

Guess who that someone is. That's right, little ol' you. And how are you going to tame that promise—that dream—to your will? A little ol' thing called—are you ready?—self-discipline.

Oh, no! Not that be-a-responsible-person thing again!

> # A journey of a thousand miles begins with a single step.
>
> ## (THE WAY OF LAO TZU)

Yup. That's the way it works. It's the price tag on leadership—including self-leadership.

Every Bird-in-the-Hand Begins with a Plan

1

Pick five areas in your life that lack discipline. Always late for school? Never finish a project? Speak before you think? Make snap judgments about people? You get the idea.

2

Decide which one you'll tackle first. (Your old friend—priorities!)

3

Jump in and do it. Get to work on just that one—and really work on it. Get some books and tapes on the subject. Watch, or ask, someone who's already nailed it.

4

Keep score. Spend fifteen minutes each morning focusing on your goal. Do a five-minute checkup on your schedule at lunch. And take another five minutes every night to ask yourself how you're doing. You could make this part of your quiet time with God.

5

Take your time. Give yourself sixty days on that one area before you move on to the next.

6

Look in the mirror, and smile. Because you're going to like that new, improved you who's looking back!

Oh, and one more thing . . .

DON'T FORGET TO GET

Just kidding. Leadership has already taught you what organization is all about—and how beautifully smooth it makes things go. Like Christopher Robin in Winnie the Pooh, you perfectly understand that: "Organizing is what you do before you do something, so that when you do it, it's not all mixed up." Makes perfect sense when you think about it, right?

Hey, Who's in Charge Here?

Who's going to make your choices . . . dream your dreams . . . create your future, if not you? It is *your* life, after all. Shouldn't you be the one in control of where it's going, what it will become?

Thought so.

So you'll probably want to get going on turning your life—and yourself—into everything you want it to be. And for that, there's no time like the present. Now. Right this minute. What are you waiting for?

Slip into Your Sneakers!

You'll want to tread lightly and carefully here. Approaching a major goal is best done with surefooted patience, one step at a time. Remember, you're not going for an amazing overnight transformation. You're going **to start small—very small,** with a very doable plan. In short, you're going to sneak up on *yourself!* You're going to start changing habits—and getting results—before that "sounds-like-a-lot-of-work" you has a chance to notice. And by then, *all* of

"LIVES OF GREAT MEN ALL REMIND US WE CAN MAKE OUR LIVES SUBLIME, AND, DEPARTING, LEAVE BEHIND US FOOTPRINTS ON THE SANDS OF TIME."
—HENRY WADSWORTH LONGFELLOW, THE MOST FAMOUS AND MOST POPULAR AMERICAN POET OF THE 1800s

you is going to like the feel of success so much you'll want more!

So here you are, organized, prioritized, and energized. What more could you possibly need to master this self-discipline thing? Well, *this* might be helpful . . .

Keep Your Chin Up, That's How You See the Stars!

Is your quest for self-discipline always going to be easy? Will it go like clockwork, with nary a hitch?

You already know the answer, don't you? If there's one thing leadership has taught you, it's that there are always hitches, glitches, and assorted bumps in the road. But you've also learned how to deal with them—by keeping your focus on the results you're working for.

What you're doing here is *not* easy. But the rewards . . . ah, the rewards . . . are almost beyond measure.

By taking charge of—by accepting responsibility for—yourself and what you become, you are working *with* God. You are using all the beautiful gifts He gave you to become what He intends. You are making yourself ready to leave His mark—and yours—on the world! What's a little effort compared to that?

Don't Forget to Enjoy Yourself!

Life—your life—is a grand adventure, planned with infinite care by the One who hung the stars and counted every grain of sand. Would He have left out joy?

Your special, one-of-a-kind life is a loving Father's gift to a precious child.

☐ Accept it with delight.

☐ Handle it with care.

☐ Fill it with joy.   ☐ Honor its gifts.

☐ Dream your dreams.

☐ Make them come true.

☐ Spread your wings and fly!

YOU HAVE BRAINS IN YOUR HEAD.
YOU HAVE FEET IN YOUR SHOES.
YOU CAN STEER YOURSELF
ANY DIRECTION YOU CHOOSE.

—DR. SEUSS, FROM
OH, THE PLACES YOU'LL GO!